# THE MILLIONAIRE MINDSET

## HOW TO THINK AND ACT LIKE THE RICH

**DAMI JOSH**

# Copyright © 2024 by Dami Josh

All rights reserved. No part of this book may be reproduced, stored in a retrieval system, or transmitted, in any form or by any means, electronic, mechanical, photocopying, recording, or otherwise, without the prior written permission of the author, except in the case of brief quotations embodied in critical reviews and certain other noncommercial uses permitted by copyright law.

# TABLE OF CONTENT

# INTRODUCTION

Welcome to "The Millionaire Mindset: How to Think and Act like the Rich," a transformative guide that unveils the secrets of achieving financial success and adopting the mindset of the wealthy. In a world where opportunities abound, understanding and cultivating the right mindset is the key to unlocking the doors to prosperity.

This book is not just about accumulating wealth; it's a roadmap to reshape your thinking, habits, and approach towards money. Drawing inspiration from successful individuals who have attained financial abundance, "The Millionaire Mindset" delves into the core principles that separate the affluent from the average. Whether you're an aspiring entrepreneur, a seasoned professional, or someone navigating the complexities of personal finance, this book offers invaluable insights to propel you towards a life of abundance.

Through a blend of practical strategies, real-life examples, and psychological principles, this guide explores how successful individuals think, make decisions, and navigate challenges. It goes beyond mere financial advice, addressing the importance of resilience, innovation, and adaptability in today's dynamic economic landscape. The book is not just about amassing wealth; it's a holistic approach to fostering a mindset that attracts success in various aspects of life.

As you journey through the pages of "The Millionaire Mindset," you'll discover actionable steps to shift your perspective, overcome limiting beliefs, and develop the resilience needed to weather financial storms. The aim is to empower you to create and sustain wealth, not just for yourself but for generations to come.

Whether you're aiming for financial independence, entrepreneurship, or a fulfilling career, this book provides the tools to cultivate a mindset that aligns with success. It's time to break free from conventional thinking and embrace the principles that have propelled countless individuals to financial greatness. Get ready to embark on a transformative journey towards the millionaire mindset and unlock the doors to a future of unlimited possibilities.

# CHAPTER 1: UNVEILING THE MILLIONAIRE MINDSET

Welcome to the gateway of transformation – Chapter 1: "Unveiling the Millionaire Mindset." In this pivotal section of our journey, we delve deep into the intricate layers of the mindset that separates the prosperous from the average. Like a master key unlocking the doors to financial success, this chapter peels back the curtain on the psychological landscape of the affluent.

Here, we embark on a fascinating exploration of the underlying principles and thought patterns that define the millionaire mindset. By dissecting the intricacies of how successful individuals perceive wealth, make decisions, and overcome obstacles, we set the stage for a profound shift in your mental framework.

The journey begins with an exploration of the psychology of wealth – an examination of the beliefs and attitudes that underpin financial success. As we navigate this terrain, we'll identify and dismantle the limiting beliefs that may have unconsciously held you back, paving the way for a mindset of abundance.

We then venture into the realm of positive and abundance-oriented thinking, recognizing its power to shape not only financial success but also overall life satisfaction. From strategic planning and goal setting to embracing risk and cultivating an entrepreneurial spirit, we uncover the core principles that successful individuals utilize in their journey towards prosperity.

Join me on this enlightening expedition as we unravel the mysteries of the millionaire mindset. Prepare to challenge your assumptions, expand your perspectives, and lay the foundation for a mindset that attracts success in all aspects of life. The unveiling has begun – are you ready to step into the realm of limitless possibilities?

# - The Psychology of Wealth

The psychology of wealth is a complex and multifaceted aspect of understanding how individuals think about and relate to money, success, and abundance. It encompasses a range of cognitive, emotional, and behavioral factors that influence financial decision-making, goal-setting, and overall well-being. Here's a comprehensive discussion on the psychology of wealth:

1. **Beliefs and Mindsets:**

   **- Limiting Beliefs:** The psychology of wealth often begins with identifying and overcoming limiting beliefs—deep-seated thoughts that hinder financial growth. These can include notions about scarcity, unworthiness, or fear of success.

Overcoming these beliefs is crucial in cultivating a mindset conducive to wealth creation.

- **Abundance Mindset:** Contrary to a scarcity mindset, an abundance mindset involves viewing the world as a place of limitless opportunities. Those with an abundance mindset believe in their ability to create wealth, attract success, and share prosperity.

2. Behavioral Economics:

- **Decision-Making Biases:** Behavioral economics explores how cognitive biases influence financial decisions. Common biases include loss aversion, where individuals fear losses more than they value gains, and present bias, leading people to prioritize short-term rewards over long-term benefits.

- **Herd Mentality:** The psychology of wealth is also affected by social dynamics, as individuals often make financial decisions based on the actions of others. Herd mentality can lead to market bubbles or crashes, highlighting the impact of social influence on financial behavior.

### 3. Financial Goal-Setting:

- **Goal Orientation:** Understanding one's financial goals is a crucial aspect of the psychology of wealth. Whether focused on achieving financial independence, entrepreneurial success, or philanthropy, individuals with clear goals are more likely to make informed financial decisions aligned with their objectives.

- **Delayed Gratification:** The ability to delay gratification is linked to long-term financial success. Those who can resist immediate rewards in favor of future gains demonstrate a psychological trait essential for wealth accumulation.

### 4. Emotional Intelligence:

- **Handling Success and Failure:** Emotional intelligence plays a significant role in how individuals respond to financial success and setbacks. Those with high emotional intelligence navigate challenges with resilience, learning from failures and avoiding the pitfalls of excessive overconfidence during success.

- **Money and Happiness:** The psychology of wealth also explores the relationship between money and happiness. While financial stability is essential for well-being, the pursuit of wealth for its own sake may not necessarily lead to lasting happiness. Understanding this balance is key to a psychologically healthy approach to wealth.

## 5. Generosity and Philanthropy:

- **The Joy of Giving:** Examining the psychology of wealth involves recognizing the impact of generosity and philanthropy on overall satisfaction. Studies suggest that individuals who engage in charitable activities often experience a sense of purpose and fulfilment, contributing to a positive psychological state.

- **Legacy Building:** For many, wealth is not just about personal success but also leaving a lasting legacy. The psychology of wealth considers how individuals view the intergenerational impact of their financial decisions, shaping their approach to legacy building.

In conclusion, the psychology of wealth is a rich and intricate field that goes beyond mere financial management. It involves understanding the deep-seated beliefs, biases, emotions, and behaviors that influence financial decisions. By exploring and mastering the psychology of wealth, individuals can cultivate a mindset that not only attracts financial success but also promotes overall well-being and fulfillment.

## - Identifying and Overcoming Limiting Beliefs

Identifying and overcoming limiting beliefs is a crucial step in personal development and achieving success, particularly in the realm of financial endeavors. Limiting beliefs are deeply ingrained thoughts or convictions that constrain an individual's potential, hinder progress, and create barriers to achieving their goals. Here's a comprehensive discussion on the process of identifying and overcoming limiting beliefs:

1. **Self-Reflection and Awareness:**

- **Recognizing Limiting Beliefs:** The journey begins with self-reflection to identify limiting beliefs. This involves introspection to pinpoint negative thought patterns or self-sabotaging beliefs that may have been formed due to past experiences, societal influences, or family upbringing.

- **Journaling and Mindfulness:** Keeping a journal and practicing mindfulness can help individuals become more aware of their thoughts and emotions. By observing thought patterns and emotional reactions, individuals can uncover limiting beliefs that may be holding them back.

2. **Challenging Assumptions:**

- **Questioning Beliefs:** Once identified, the next step is to question the validity of these limiting beliefs. Individuals need to challenge their assumptions and ask themselves whether these beliefs are based on facts or unfounded perceptions.

- **Examining Evidence:** Seeking evidence that supports or contradicts limiting beliefs is a powerful strategy. Often, individuals discover that their beliefs are not grounded in reality but are distorted interpretations of past events.

### 3. Cognitive Restructuring:

- **Replacing Negative Thoughts:** Cognitive restructuring involves replacing negative and limiting thoughts with positive and empowering ones. This process requires individuals to consciously choose alternative, more constructive beliefs that align with their goals and aspirations.

- **Affirmations:** Using positive affirmations is a practical tool for reinforcing new beliefs. By consistently repeating positive statements, individuals can reprogram their subconscious mind and gradually replace limiting beliefs with empowering ones.

4. **Seeking External Support:**

- Therapy and Coaching: Professional guidance, such as therapy or coaching, can provide valuable support in identifying and overcoming limiting beliefs. Therapists and coaches use various techniques to help individuals explore and address the root causes of their limiting beliefs.

- **Peer Support:** Sharing thoughts and experiences with trusted friends, mentors, or support groups can offer an external perspective. Sometimes, discussing limiting beliefs with others provides insights and encouragement to challenge and overcome them.

5. **Behavioral Changes:**

- **Taking Small Steps:** Overcoming limiting beliefs often involves taking small, manageable steps outside one's comfort zone. Success in these incremental actions helps build confidence and gradually dismantles the belief that certain goals are unattainable.

**- Celebrating Achievements:** Acknowledging and celebrating even minor achievements reinforces the process of overcoming limiting beliefs. Positive reinforcement contributes to the establishment of a new, empowering mindset.

## 6. Consistent Practice:

**- Daily Habits:** The process of overcoming limiting beliefs requires consistent effort. Engaging in daily practices, such as positive visualization, goal-setting, and gratitude exercises, reinforces the new belief system and creates a positive mental environment.

**- Lifelong Learning:** Embracing a mindset of continuous learning and growth is crucial. Individuals should remain open to new experiences, perspectives, and information that challenge and reshape their beliefs throughout their personal and professional journeys.

In conclusion, identifying and overcoming limiting beliefs is a transformative process that involves self-awareness, challenging assumptions, cognitive restructuring, seeking support, making behavioral changes, and maintaining the consistent effort. By actively addressing these beliefs, individuals can break free from self-imposed constraints and open themselves to a world of possibilities, particularly in the pursuit of financial success and overall well-being.

## - Cultivating a Positive and Abundance-Oriented Mindset

Cultivating a positive and abundance-oriented mindset is a transformative process that involves shifting one's thoughts, attitudes, and beliefs to focus on possibilities, gratitude, and the inherent abundance of life. This mindset is foundational for achieving success, overcoming challenges, and fostering overall well-being. Here's a comprehensive discussion on the process of cultivating a positive and abundance-oriented mindset:

1. **Self-Reflection:**

- Awareness of Current Mindset: The first step in cultivating a positive mindset is self-reflection. Individuals need to become aware of their current thought patterns, identifying any negative or scarcity-based beliefs that may be hindering their progress.

- **Understanding the Power of Thoughts:** Recognizing that thoughts have a profound impact on emotions, behaviors, and outcomes is crucial. Understanding this connection empowers individuals to take control of their thought processes.

2. **Gratitude Practice:**

- **Daily Gratitude Journaling:** Cultivating an abundance mindset often begins with gratitude. Keeping a daily journal to acknowledge and appreciate positive aspects of life helps shift the focus from what is lacking to what is present and valuable.

- **Expressing Gratitude:** Actively expressing gratitude to others, whether through written notes or verbal communication, reinforces positive connections and contributes to a sense of abundance in relationships.

### 3. Positive Affirmations:

- **Affirming Positive Beliefs:** Positive affirmations involve consciously and repeatedly affirming positive beliefs about oneself and one's capabilities. These affirmations help rewire the subconscious mind, fostering a more optimistic and confident mindset.

- **Aligning Affirmations with Goals:** Tailoring affirmations to align with specific goals amplifies their effectiveness. By affirming success, abundance, and capability, individuals program their minds to focus on opportunities rather than obstacles.

### 4. Visualization Techniques:

- **Creative Visualization:** Visualization involves mentally picturing oneself achieving goals and living a life of abundance. This technique helps create a vivid mental image of success, making it more tangible and attainable.

   - **Future Self-Visualization**: Envisioning one's future self-enjoying success and abundance creates a positive expectancy. This mental rehearsal can enhance motivation and resilience in the face of challenges.

5.  **Mindful Awareness:**

   - **Present Moment Focus:** Mindfulness encourages individuals to focus on the present moment without judgment. By cultivating awareness of thoughts and emotions in the now, individuals can prevent negative thinking patterns from taking over.

   - **Non-Attachment to Outcomes:** An abundance-oriented mindset involves embracing uncertainty and being open to various outcomes. Non-attachment to specific results reduces anxiety and allows individuals to adapt more flexibly to changing circumstances.

6. **Surrounding Oneself with Positivity:**

- **Positive Influences:** Engaging with positive influences, whether through relationships, media, or social environments, contributes to a more optimistic mindset. Surrounding oneself with positivity reinforces the belief in abundance.

- **Limiting Negative Inputs:** Minimizing exposure to negative news, toxic relationships, or self-critical thoughts helps maintain a positive mental environment. Conscious choices in this regard support the cultivation of an abundance-oriented mindset.

7. **Continuous Learning and Growth:**

- **Embracing Challenges as Opportunities:** A growth mindset views challenges as opportunities for learning and improvement. Embracing setbacks with resilience and a positive attitude fosters ongoing personal and professional development.

**- Curiosity and Open-Mindedness:** Cultivating a positive mindset involves staying curious, open-minded, and willing to explore new possibilities. This approach encourages a mindset of abundance by recognizing the vast potential for growth and expansion.

In conclusion, cultivating a positive and abundance-oriented mindset is a dynamic and ongoing process that involves self-reflection, gratitude practices, positive affirmations, visualization, mindfulness, positive influences, and a commitment to continuous learning and growth. By actively engaging in these practices, individuals can reshape their mindset, foster a sense of abundance, and navigate life's challenges with optimism and resilience.

# CHAPTER 2: THINKING LIKE THE RICH: CORE PRINCIPLES OF FINANCIAL SUCCESS

Welcome to the transformative exploration of Chapter 2: "Thinking like the Rich - Core Principles of Financial Success." In this pivotal chapter, we embark on a journey into the mindset of those who have mastered the art of wealth creation. It's not just about accumulating riches; it's about understanding and embracing the core principles that guide successful individuals in their pursuit of financial abundance.

Here, we unravel the secrets behind strategic thinking, goal setting, and the entrepreneurial spirit that propels the affluent toward sustained success. "Thinking like the Rich" is more than a mere observation of financial behavior; it's an invitation to adopt a mindset that transcends traditional approaches and propels you towards a future of unparalleled prosperity.

As we delve into this chapter, we'll dissect the fundamental principles that define the thought processes of the financially successful. From the meticulous planning of strategic goals to the bold embrace of risk and innovation, each principle is a building block in the architecture of wealth creation.

Get ready to challenge your existing notions, break free from conventional thinking, and adopt a mindset that aligns with the essence of financial success. Whether you're an aspiring entrepreneur, a seasoned professional, or someone navigating the complexities of personal finance, "Thinking like the Rich" offers a roadmap to not only understand but embody the core principles that underpin the financial triumphs of the affluent.

Let this chapter be your guide to thinking strategically, setting audacious goals, and embracing the mindset that turns dreams into reality. As we navigate through these pages, may you find inspiration and practical insights that propel you towards a life defined by financial abundance and success? Welcome to the realm of thinking like the rich, where possibilities are limitless, and the pursuit of prosperity becomes an art form.

# - Strategic Planning and Goal Setting

Strategic planning and goal setting are critical components of achieving success in various aspects of life, especially in the pursuit of financial prosperity. These processes provide a roadmap for individuals and organizations, guiding them toward their objectives with purpose and efficiency. Here's a comprehensive discussion on strategic planning and goal setting:

1. **Strategic Planning:**

  - **Definition and Purpose:** Strategic planning is a systematic process of defining an organization's or individual's direction and making decisions on allocating its resources to pursue this direction. It involves setting priorities, focusing energy and resources, and ensuring that everyone is working toward common goals.

- **Long-Term Vision:** Central to strategic planning is the creation of a long-term vision. This vision serves as a guiding star, outlining where an individual or organization wants to be in the future. It provides a sense of purpose and helps in aligning day-to-day activities with overarching objectives.

- **SWOT Analysis:** Strategic planning often includes a comprehensive SWOT analysis, which assesses an entity's Strengths, Weaknesses, Opportunities, and Threats. This analysis informs the development of strategies that leverage strengths, mitigate weaknesses, capitalize on opportunities, and address potential threats.

- **Resource Allocation:** Strategic planning involves allocating resources effectively and efficiently. This includes financial resources, human capital, time, and technology. Proper allocation ensures that efforts are focused on activities that contribute most to the achievement of strategic goals.

## 2. Goal Setting:

- **Definition and Importance:** Goal setting is the process of defining specific, measurable, achievable, relevant, and time-bound (SMART) objectives that an individual or organization aims to accomplish. Clear goals provide direction, motivation, and a benchmark for measuring progress.

- **Short-Term and Long-Term Goals:** Goals can be categorized as short-term and long-term. Short-term goals provide immediate direction and motivation, while long-term goals contribute to the overall vision. A balance between the two ensures a dynamic and strategic approach to achievement.

- **Alignment with Vision:** Goals should be aligned with the long-term vision established through strategic planning. This ensures that every short-term objective contributes to the larger purpose and moves an individual or organization closer to its desired future state.

- **Measuring Progress:** Establishing key performance indicators (KPIs) and milestones is essential for tracking progress toward goals. Regular assessment and adjustments help ensure that objectives remain relevant and achievable.

3. **Integration of Strategic Planning and Goal Setting:**

- **Coherence:** Strategic planning and goal setting are interconnected processes that reinforce each other. The overarching strategy guides the establishment of goals, ensuring they are aligned with the broader vision. Goals, in turn, contribute to the execution of the strategy.

- **Adaptability:** While strategic plans provide a framework, they should also be adaptable to changing circumstances. Goal setting allows for flexibility, enabling individuals or organizations to recalibrate their objectives based on evolving needs, opportunities, or challenges.

   - **Communication and Collaboration:** The integration of strategic planning and goal setting facilitates effective communication and collaboration. Everyone involved understands the broader strategy and how their specific goals contribute to the collective success, fostering a sense of shared purpose.

## 4.  Continuous Improvement:

   - **Feedback Mechanisms:** Both strategic planning and goal setting benefit from feedback mechanisms. Regular evaluations, performance reviews, and assessments provide insights into what is working well and where adjustments are needed. This iterative process contributes to continuous improvement.

   - **Learning from Experience:** Learning from both successes and failures is crucial in refining future strategic plans and goals. It encourages adaptability, resilience, and a commitment to ongoing growth and development.

5. **Implementation and Execution:**

- **Actionable Plans:** Effective strategic planning and goal setting lead to actionable plans. These plans outline specific steps, responsibilities, and timelines for executing strategies and achieving goals.

- **Monitoring and Adaptation:** Implementation involves monitoring progress against the plan and making necessary adaptations. This requires a proactive approach to address challenges, capitalize on opportunities, and ensure that the overall trajectory aligns with the established strategic vision.

In conclusion, strategic planning and goal setting are inseparable elements in the pursuit of success, especially in the context of financial prosperity. They provide structure, direction, and purpose, guiding individuals and organizations toward their desired future states. Through a dynamic and integrated approach, these processes foster adaptability, continuous improvement, and a resilient mindset necessary for navigating the complexities of personal and professional endeavors.

## - Embracing Risk and Entrepreneurial Thinking

Embracing risk and adopting entrepreneurial thinking are crucial components for individuals seeking financial success and navigating dynamic business environments. This mindset involves a willingness to take calculated risks, identify opportunities, and innovate in the pursuit of goals. Here's a comprehensive discussion on the process of embracing risk and entrepreneurial thinking:

1. **Understanding Risk:**

   - **Definition:** Risk refers to the potential for loss or failure. Embracing risk involves recognizing that taking calculated risks is an inherent part of any venture, and avoiding risk altogether can limit potential rewards.

   - **Risk Tolerance:** Individuals need to assess and understand their risk tolerance. This involves evaluating their capacity to withstand potential setbacks and uncertainties, both financially and emotionally.

   - **Risk vs. Reward:** Entrepreneurial thinking involves weighing the potential rewards against the associated risks. This strategic evaluation helps in making informed decisions about whether a risk is worth taking.

2.  **Cultivating an Entrepreneurial Mindset:**

   - **Opportunity Recognition:** Entrepreneurial thinking involves actively seeking and recognizing opportunities. This mindset looks beyond challenges and focuses on identifying gaps in the market, emerging trends, or areas for improvement.

- **Innovation:** Entrepreneurs thrive on innovation. They seek creative solutions to problems and are willing to disrupt traditional approaches to finding more efficient or effective ways of doing things.

- **Adaptability:** Embracing risk requires adaptability. Entrepreneurs are open to change, and they quickly adjust their strategies in response to feedback, market shifts, or unexpected challenges.

3. **Risk Management:**

- **Calculated Risk-Taking:** Entrepreneurial thinking doesn't mean reckless risk-taking. It involves taking calculated risks by thoroughly assessing potential outcomes, developing contingency plans, and understanding the probabilities associated with different scenarios.

- **Diversification:** Entrepreneurs often diversify their ventures or investments to spread risk. Diversification can help mitigate the impact of failures in one area by having multiple streams of income or projects.

- **Continuous Learning:** Entrepreneurs embrace a culture of continuous learning. They use past experiences, whether successes or failures, as opportunities for growth and refinement of their risk management strategies.

4. **Failure as a Learning Opportunity:**

- **Reframing Failure:** Entrepreneurial thinking views failure as a learning opportunity rather than an outcome. Failures provide valuable insights and experiences that contribute to personal and professional growth.

- **Iterative Process:** Entrepreneurs understand that success often comes through an iterative process of trial and error. Each failure provides feedback and informs adjustments, bringing them closer to achieving their goals.

- **Resilience:** A crucial aspect of embracing risk is developing resilience. Entrepreneurs bounce back from setbacks, viewing challenges as temporary obstacles rather than insurmountable barriers.

5. **Creating a Risk-Taking Culture:**

- **Encouraging Innovation:** In an entrepreneurial environment, there's a focus on encouraging and rewarding innovative thinking. This fosters a culture where individuals feel empowered to take calculated risks in the pursuit of novel ideas.

- **Open Communication:** A culture that embraces risk promotes open communication. Individuals should feel comfortable expressing ideas, sharing concerns, and collaborating on solutions without fear of punitive measures for taking risks.

- **Rewarding Initiative:** Recognizing and rewarding initiative and risk-taking behaviors reinforces an entrepreneurial mindset. This could be through incentives, promotions, or acknowledgement of contributions to the organization's success.

6. **Networking and Collaboration:**

- **Building a Support System:** Entrepreneurs understand the value of networking and collaboration. Establishing a supportive network provides access to resources, mentorship, and diverse perspectives that can help mitigate risks.

- **Partnerships:** Collaborative efforts and partnerships can distribute risks among multiple parties. Entrepreneurs explore opportunities for mutually beneficial collaborations that enhance their ability to tackle challenges and seize opportunities.

7. **Continuous Evaluation and Adaptation:**

- **Feedback Loops:** Entrepreneurs create feedback loops to continuously evaluate the outcomes of their decisions. Regular assessments help in identifying areas for improvement, refining strategies, and adapting to changing circumstances.

- **Pivoting:** Entrepreneurial thinking involves a willingness to pivot when necessary. If a particular approach or venture is not yielding the expected results, entrepreneurs are open to changing direction based on the insights gained from their experiences.

In conclusion, the process of embracing risk and adopting entrepreneurial thinking is a dynamic and strategic endeavor. It involves understanding risk, cultivating an entrepreneurial mindset, managing risk effectively, viewing failure as an opportunity to learn, and creating a risk-taking culture, leveraging networking and collaboration, and continuously evaluating and adapting strategies. Embracing risk is not about reckless behavior but about making informed decisions that propel individuals toward innovation, growth, and ultimately, financial success.

## - Developing a Long-Term Wealth Building Strategy

Developing a long-term wealth-building strategy is a systematic and intentional process that involves setting financial goals, making informed decisions, and adopting sustainable practices to accumulate and preserve wealth over an extended period. Here's a comprehensive discussion on the process of developing a long-term wealth-building strategy:

1.  **Define Financial Goals:**

   - **Clarity and Specificity:** The first step is to define clear and specific financial goals. Whether it's saving for retirement, buying a home, funding education, or achieving financial independence, well-defined objectives provide direction and motivation.

   - **Short-Term and Long-Term Objectives:** Distinguish between short-term and long-term goals. Short-term goals may include building an emergency fund, while long-term goals involve substantial wealth accumulation over an extended period.

2.  **Assess Current Financial Situation:**

   - **Income and Expenses:** Evaluate current income and expenses to understand the available resources for wealth building. Identifying areas for saving and optimizing spending habits is crucial.

- **Debt Assessment:** Assess existing debts and develop a plan for debt reduction. Reducing high-interest debt can free up resources for investment and wealth-building activities.

- **Net worth Calculation:** Calculate net worth by subtracting liabilities from assets. Regularly tracking net worth provides insights into overall financial progress.

3. **Risk Tolerance and Investment Strategy:**

- **Risk Assessment:** Understand personal risk tolerance by evaluating the ability to withstand market fluctuations. Assessing risk tolerance helps in creating an investment strategy aligned with individual comfort levels.

- **Diversification:** Develop an investment portfolio that aligns with long-term goals and risk tolerance. Diversification, spreading investments across different asset classes, helps manage risk and optimize returns.

- **Regular Review:** Periodically review and adjust the investment strategy based on changing financial goals, market conditions, and risk tolerance.

4. **Emergency Fund and Insurance:**

- **Establish Emergency Fund:** Building a robust emergency fund is crucial for financial resilience. Aim for three to six months' worth of living expenses in a liquid and easily accessible account.

- **Insurance Coverage:** Ensure adequate insurance coverage for health, life, property, and other relevant areas. Insurance protects against unforeseen events and provides financial security for the long term.

5. **Tax Planning:**

- **Tax-Efficient Strategies:** Develop tax-efficient strategies to optimize income and reduce tax liabilities. Utilize tax-advantaged accounts such as retirement accounts, Health Savings Accounts (HSAs), and other tax-efficient investment vehicles.

- **Professional Advice:** Seek professional advice from tax experts or financial advisors to navigate complex tax regulations and leverage available tax incentives.

## 6. Retirement Planning:

- **Retirement Goals:** Clearly define retirement goals, considering lifestyle expectations, healthcare expenses, and potential longevity. Develop a retirement savings plan tailored to meet these objectives.

- **Regular Contributions:** Consistently contribute to retirement accounts, taking advantage of employer-sponsored plans and individual retirement accounts (IRAs). Consider maximizing contributions to benefit from compounding over time.

## 7. Education Planning:

- **Educational Goals:** If education funding is a goal, create a plan for saving and investing. Utilize tax-advantaged education savings accounts like 529 plans to build a dedicated fund for educational expenses.

- **Start Early:** Start saving for education as early as possible to benefit from the compounding effect and reduce the financial burden when educational expenses arise.

8.  **Real Estate and Business Ventures:**

- **Strategic Real Estate Investments:** Consider real estate investments as part of the wealth-building strategy. Real estate can provide both passive income and appreciation over time.

- **Entrepreneurial Ventures:** Explore entrepreneurial opportunities or business ventures as a means of building wealth. Entrepreneurs can create value and generate significant returns through successful business endeavors.

9.  **Continuous Learning and Adaptation:**

- **Stay Informed:** Keep abreast of financial markets, economic trends, and investment opportunities. Stay informed about changes in tax laws, retirement regulations, and other factors that may impact the wealth-building strategy.

   **- Adapt to Changing Circumstances:** Life circumstances change, and the wealth-building strategy should adapt accordingly. Regularly reassess financial goals and adjust the strategy to align with evolving priorities and economic conditions.

### 10.  Estate Planning:

   **- Legacy and Wealth Transfer:** Develop an estate plan that addresses wealth transfer, minimizing tax implications and ensuring that assets are distributed according to personal wishes.

   **- Professional Assistance:** Seek legal advice and assistance from estate planning professionals to create a comprehensive plan that safeguards assets and provides for future generations.

In conclusion, developing a long-term wealth-building strategy is a comprehensive process that involves setting clear goals, assessing the current financial situation, managing risks, making informed investments, and adapting to changing circumstances. It requires discipline, continuous learning, and a commitment to the long-term vision. A well-crafted wealth-building strategy not only accumulates financial assets but also provides a foundation for financial security and the realization of personal and generational aspirations.

# CHAPTER 3: HABITS OF THE WEALTHY: ACTIONS THAT LEAD TO PROSPERITY

Welcome to the illuminating journey of Chapter 3: "Habits of the Wealthy - Actions That Lead to Prosperity." In this chapter, we delve into the daily routines, behaviors, and choices that distinguish the financially successful from the rest. These habits are the building blocks of prosperity, shaping the trajectory of individuals who have mastered the art of wealth creation.

As we navigate through these pages, we'll unravel the secrets behind the habits that contribute to sustained financial success. It's not merely about luck or one-time achievements; it's about ingrained behaviors and choices that cultivate a mindset conducive to prosperity.

From disciplined financial practices to effective time management, "Habits of the Wealthy" explores the rituals that set the affluent apart. Whether you're an aspiring entrepreneur, a seasoned professional, or someone on the path to financial independence, this chapter serves as a guide to adopt and integrate habits that lead to long-term prosperity.

Prepare to witness the unveiling of strategies that extend beyond the boardroom and into everyday life. The habits discussed here are not isolated actions but interconnected threads that weave a tapestry of success. Each habit is a conscious choice, a repeated action that contributes to the accumulation and preservation of wealth.

Join me on this enlightening exploration as we uncover the key habits that empower individuals to create and sustain prosperity. Let this chapter be a source of inspiration and practical insights, guiding you towards a life enriched by the habits that pave the way for financial abundance. Welcome to the realm of "Habits of the Wealthy," where actions transform into prosperity, and prosperity becomes a way of life.

## - The Power of Consistency in Financial Habits

The power of consistency in financial habits is a fundamental principle that underlies long-term success and wealth-building. Consistency involves regularly practicing positive financial behaviors and making disciplined choices over time. This consistency not only helps individuals achieve their financial goals but also establishes a strong foundation for financial security and prosperity. Here's a comprehensive discussion on the power of consistency in financial habits:

1. **Budgeting and Spending Habits:**

   - **Consistent Budgeting:** Creating and adhering to a budget is a cornerstone of financial stability. Consistency in budgeting ensures that individuals are aware of their income, expenses, and financial priorities, enabling better control over their financial well-being.

- **Mindful Spending:** Consistently practicing mindful spending involves making intentional and informed choices about where money is allocated. Avoiding impulsive purchases and staying committed to financial goals contribute to long-term financial success.

2.  **Savings and Emergency Funds:**

- **Regular Saving:** The power of consistency is evident in regular savings habits. Consistently setting aside a portion of income for savings, whether for short-term goals or emergency funds, allows for the accumulation of financial reserves over time.

- **Emergency Fund Contributions:** Regular contributions to an emergency fund provide a financial safety net, ensuring individuals are prepared for unexpected expenses without disrupting their long-term financial plans.

3. **Investing and Wealth Building:**

  - **Consistent Investment Contributions:** The power of compound interest is maximized through consistent contributions to investment accounts. Regularly investing, even in small amounts, allows individuals to benefit from compounding and the potential for long-term capital growth.

  - **Diversification Strategies:** Consistently applying diversification strategies in investment portfolios helps spread risk and enhance the potential for returns. Regularly reviewing and rebalancing the portfolio ensures alignment with financial goals and risk tolerance.

4. **Debt Management:**

  - **Consistent Debt Repayment:** Managing debt consistently involves making regular payments and developing a strategy for debt reduction. Consistency in debt repayment contributes to improved credit scores and financial well-being.

- **Avoiding Accumulation:** Consistency in financial habits includes avoiding the accumulation of high-interest debt. This involves responsible use of credit and making informed decisions to prevent debt from becoming a burden.

5. **Financial Education and Planning:**

- **Continuous Learning:** Consistently investing time in financial education enhances individuals' understanding of personal finance. Staying informed about economic trends, investment strategies, and financial planning contributes to better decision-making.

- **Long-Term Planning**: Consistent long-term financial planning involves regularly assessing financial goals, adjusting strategies based on changing circumstances, and adapting to evolving life priorities.

6. **Career Development and Income Growth:**

- **Skill Enhancement:** Consistently developing skills and staying relevant in one's career contributes to income growth. The power of consistency in professional development ensures individuals are positioned for advancement and increased earning potential.

**- Negotiating and Seeking Opportunities:** Consistently seeking opportunities for career advancement, negotiating salary increases, and exploring additional income streams contribute to long-term financial success.

### 7. Retirement Planning:

**- Regular Contributions to Retirement Accounts:** Consistency in contributing to retirement accounts, such as 401(k)s or IRAs, is crucial for building a substantial retirement nest egg. Regular contributions over an extended period maximize the benefits of compounding.

**- Reviewing Retirement Plans:** Consistently reviewing and adjusting retirement plans ensures they remain aligned with evolving financial goals, lifestyle expectations, and changing economic conditions.

8. **Mindset and Financial Discipline:**

- **Building Financial Discipline:** Consistency builds financial discipline by instilling positive habits that become routine. Over time, financial discipline becomes ingrained, making it easier to resist impulsive decisions that may jeopardize long-term goals.

- **Cultivating a Growth Mindset:** Consistency fosters a growth mindset, encouraging individuals to view financial challenges as opportunities for learning and improvement. This mindset promotes resilience and adaptability in the face of setbacks.

9. **Legacy Planning:**

- **Consistent Estate Planning:** Legacy planning involves consistent efforts in creating and updating wills, trusts, and other estate planning documents. Regular reviews ensure that the plan aligns with changing family dynamics, financial circumstances, and legal considerations.

**- Intergenerational Wealth Transfer:**
Consistency in teaching financial principles to the next generation and fostering a culture of responsible financial habits contributes to intergenerational wealth transfer.

In conclusion, the power of consistency in financial habits lies in the cumulative impact of small, repeated actions over time. By consistently practicing positive financial behaviors, individuals can build resilience, achieve financial goals, and ultimately pave the way for long-term prosperity. Consistency transforms financial habits into a sustainable way of life, fostering a path to financial security and success.

# - Time Management and Productivity for Success

Time management and productivity are integral elements for achieving success in both personal and professional endeavors. Effectively managing time and maximizing productivity contribute to goal attainment, reduced stress, and overall well-being. Here's a comprehensive discussion on the importance of time management and productivity for success:

1. **Goal Alignment:**

   - **Clarity of Objectives:** Time management begins with a clear understanding of personal and professional goals. Clearly defined objectives help prioritize tasks and allocate time efficiently toward meaningful endeavors.

   - **Aligning Activities with Goals:** Productivity is enhanced when daily activities align with overarching goals. Time management ensures that efforts are directed toward tasks that contribute most to the achievement of desired outcomes.

2. **Prioritization and Planning:**

   - **Urgent vs. Important:** Effective time management involves distinguishing between urgent and important tasks. Prioritizing important tasks over those that seem urgent but lack significance ensures a focus on activities that drive long-term success.

- **Strategic Planning:** Productivity is optimized through strategic planning. Creating daily, weekly, and long-term plans allows for a structured approach to tasks, reducing the likelihood of time wasted on indecision or unnecessary activities.

3. **Time Blocking and Batch Processing:**

- **Time Blocking:** Allocating specific time blocks for different types of tasks enhances concentration and efficiency. Time blocking minimizes distractions, allowing individuals to immerse themselves fully in one task before moving on to the next.

- **Batch Processing:** Grouping similar tasks and processing them in batches improves productivity. This approach minimizes context-switching and allows individuals to maintain focus on specific types of activities for more extended periods.

4. **Effective Delegation:**

  - **Identifying Strengths and Weaknesses:** Time management involves recognizing personal strengths and weaknesses. Delegating tasks that align with others' strengths frees up time for individuals to focus on activities where they excel.

  - **Empowering Others:** Delegating not only reduces an individual's workload but also empowers team members by assigning responsibilities based on their expertise. This collaborative approach fosters a more productive and efficient work environment.

5. **Technology and Tools:**

  - **Effective Use of Technology:** Leveraging productivity tools, apps, and technologies enhances time management. Calendar apps, project management tools, and communication platforms streamline tasks and facilitate efficient collaboration.

- **Automation:** Automating repetitive and routine tasks reduces manual workload. Automation tools enhance productivity by handling mundane activities, allowing individuals to focus on more complex and strategic aspects of their work.

6. **Setting Realistic Deadlines:**

- **SMART Goals:** Time management involves setting Specific, Measurable, and Achievable, Relevant, and Time-bound (SMART) goals. Realistic deadlines create a sense of urgency, helping individuals stay focused and committed to completing tasks on time.

- **Avoiding Procrastination:** Procrastination is a common barrier to productivity. Setting realistic deadlines and breaking tasks into smaller, manageable steps makes it easier to overcome procrastination and maintain momentum.

7. **Continuous Learning and Skill Development:**

- **Investing Time in Learning:** Prioritizing time for continuous learning and skill development contributes to long-term success. Staying updated on industry trends, acquiring new knowledge, and enhancing skills ensures individuals remain competitive and adaptable.

- **Efficient Learning Techniques:** Adopting effective learning techniques, such as the Pomodoro Technique or active reading strategies, maximizes the retention of information. Productivity in learning enhances the application of new knowledge to tasks and projects.

## 8. Healthy Work-Life Balance:

- **Setting Boundaries:** Effective time management includes setting boundaries between work and personal life. Maintaining a healthy work-life balance prevents burnout and ensures sustained productivity over the long term.

- **Scheduled Breaks:** Productivity is optimized when individuals incorporate scheduled breaks into their workdays. Short breaks enhance focus and mental clarity, preventing fatigue and promoting overall well-being.

9. **Adaptability and Flexibility:**

   - **Embracing Change:** Time management strategies should be adaptable to changing circumstances. Embracing change and adjusting plans as needed ensures that individuals can navigate unexpected challenges without compromising productivity.

   - **Flexibility in Approach:** Productivity is not a rigid concept; it requires flexibility in approach. Individuals should be open to adjusting their strategies based on evolving priorities, external factors, and feedback.

10. **Reflecting and Evaluating:**

   - **Regular Assessments:** Time management and productivity benefit from regular self-assessment. Individuals should reflect on their time allocation, identify areas for improvement, and adjust their strategies accordingly.

- **Celebrating Achievements:** Recognizing and celebrating accomplishments, both big and small, reinforces positive habits. Acknowledging successes motivates individuals to maintain high levels of productivity and continue striving for success.

In conclusion, effective time management and productivity are essential elements for achieving success in personal and professional domains. These practices enable individuals to align their efforts with overarching goals, prioritize tasks strategically, leverage technology efficiently, and maintain a healthy work-life balance. By consistently applying these principles, individuals can enhance their effectiveness, reduce stress, and pave the way for sustained success in their endeavors.

# - Building and Leveraging Networks for Wealth Creation

Building and leveraging networks is a strategic process that plays a pivotal role in wealth creation. Networking goes beyond simple social interactions; it involves cultivating meaningful connections, accessing valuable resources, and leveraging opportunities for financial success. Here's a comprehensive discussion on the process of building and leveraging networks for wealth creation:

1.  **Identifying Goals and Objectives:**

   **- Clarifying Financial Goals:** Before building a network, individuals should have a clear understanding of their financial goals. Whether it's seeking investment opportunities, launching a business, or advancing a career, aligning networking efforts with specific objectives is crucial.

- **Defining Target Connections:** Identify the types of connections that can contribute to wealth creation. This may include potential investors, business partners, mentors, clients, or industry experts. Tailoring networking efforts to specific goals ensures efficiency and relevance.

2.  **Building a Diverse Network:**

- **Industry Connections:** Cultivate connections within one's industry to stay informed about trends, opportunities, and potential collaborations. Engaging with professionals in the same field provides insights and access to valuable resources.

- **Cross-Industry Networking:** Building a diverse network across different industries fosters creativity and exposes individuals to a broader range of opportunities. Cross-industry connections can lead to innovative solutions and partnerships.

3.  **Creating a Strong Personal Brand:**

- **Authenticity and Reputation:** Building a strong personal brand involves being authentic and consistently demonstrating expertise and integrity. A positive reputation within the network enhances credibility and trust, making individuals more attractive collaborators or partners.

- **Value Proposition:** communicate the value one brings to the network. Whether it's unique skills, industry knowledge, or a track record of success, a compelling value proposition attracts the attention of potential collaborators and investors.

4.  **Attending Networking Events:**

- **Industry Conferences and Seminars:** Actively participating in industry-specific events provides opportunities to meet like-minded professionals and potential collaborators. These events offer a platform to showcase expertise, exchange ideas, and build relationships.

**- Local Business Meetups:** Attend local business meetups or networking events to connect with professionals from diverse backgrounds. Local networks can be instrumental in identifying regional opportunities and forming partnerships.

5. **Utilizing Online Platforms:**

**- LinkedIn and Professional Networks:** Utilize online platforms like LinkedIn to expand professional networks. Regularly updating profiles, sharing insights, and engaging in industry discussions enhance visibility and attract relevant connections.

**- Online Forums and Communities:** Joining online forums and communities related to specific industries or interests provides additional networking avenues. These platforms facilitate discussions, knowledge sharing, and the discovery of potential collaborators.

6. **Building Meaningful Relationships:**

**- Investing Time in Relationships:** Networking is not just about the number of connections but the quality of relationships. Invest time in building meaningful connections by understanding others' needs and offering support when possible.

- **Networking Follow-Ups:** Regularly follow up with contacts to nurture relationships. This may involve checking in, sharing relevant information, or expressing gratitude for collaborative efforts. Consistent communication maintains the vitality of connections.

7. **Mentorship and Advisory Relationships:**

- **Seeking Mentorship:** Building relationships with mentors or advisors who have achieved success in the desired field can provide valuable guidance. Mentorship offers insights, advice, and access to a mentor's network.

- **Being a Mentor:** In addition to seeking mentorship, consider becoming a mentor to others. Mentoring fosters a sense of community, expands one's influence, and often leads to reciprocal relationships.

8. **Collaborative Projects and Ventures:**

- **Identifying Synergies:** Explore collaborative projects or ventures with network connections. Identifying synergies and complementary strengths can lead to mutually beneficial initiatives that contribute to wealth creation.

- **Pooling Resources:** Leveraging the resources within the network, such as expertise, funding, or market access, enhances the likelihood of successful collaborative ventures. Shared efforts often result in amplified outcomes.

9. **Staying Informed and Adapting:**

- **Market Trends and Opportunities:** Continuously stay informed about market trends and emerging opportunities. Networking provides a valuable source of information, and adapting strategies based on changing circumstances ensures relevance and effectiveness.

- **Networking Trends:** Stay abreast of evolving networking trends and technologies. Incorporate new tools and platforms to enhance networking efforts, especially as digital and virtual networking continue to play a significant role.

10. **Giving Back to the Network:**

- **Contributing Value:** Actively contribute value to the network by sharing insights, resources, or opportunities. Giving back fosters a sense of reciprocity and strengthens relationships within the network.

- **Supporting Others:** Supporting the goals and initiatives of others in the network builds goodwill. By being a resource and providing assistance when possible, individuals strengthen their positions as trusted and valuable members of the network.

11. **Measuring and Evaluating Network Effectiveness:**

- **Key Performance Indicators (KPIs):** Establish KPIs to measure the effectiveness of networking efforts. This may include the number of collaborations initiated, the growth of the network, or the successful execution of joint ventures.

- **Regular Evaluations:** Periodically evaluate the impact of networking on wealth creation. Assess whether the network is contributing to the achievement of financial goals and make adjustments to the networking strategy as needed.

In conclusion, the process of building and leveraging networks for wealth creation involves strategic planning, relationship-building, and continuous adaptation. A well-cultivated network provides access to opportunities, resources, and expertise that can significantly contribute to financial success. By prioritizing meaningful connections, demonstrating value, and staying attuned to market dynamics, individuals can leverage their networks as powerful assets on the journey toward wealth creation.

# CHAPTER 4: NAVIGATING CHALLENGES: RESILIENCE AND ADAPTABILITY

Welcome to Chapter 4: "Navigating Challenges - Resilience and Adaptability." In this transformative exploration, we delve into the indispensable qualities of resilience and adaptability, both essential navigational tools in the ever-changing landscapes of life and success.

Life is an unpredictable journey, marked by twists, turns, and unexpected challenges. How individuals confront and overcome adversity often determines their trajectory toward prosperity. This chapter is a compass for those navigating the sometimes turbulent waters of personal and professional challenges, shedding light on the profound impact of resilience and adaptability in the face of adversity.

Throughout these pages, we will unravel the significance of resilience, the ability to bounce back from setbacks with newfound strength, and adaptability, the capacity to adjust and thrive in dynamic circumstances. Together, these qualities form a powerful duo, empowering individuals to not only weather storms but to emerge stronger, more resourceful, and better positioned for success.

Get ready to explore stories of triumph over adversity, practical strategies for building resilience, and insights into fostering adaptability in an ever-changing world. This chapter serves as a guide, offering inspiration and actionable advice to those navigating challenges on the path to personal and financial fulfilment.

As we embark on this journey, let the wisdom within these pages be a source of empowerment, guiding you to navigate challenges with resilience, embrace change with adaptability, and ultimately emerge triumphant in the pursuit of your goals. Welcome to the transformative realm of "Navigating Challenges - Resilience and Adaptability."

# - Learning from Failure: Turning Setbacks into Success

Learning from failure is a transformative process that involves turning setbacks into stepping stones for success. Failure is an inevitable part of any journey, but how individuals respond to and learn from these setbacks often determines their ultimate success. Here's a comprehensive discussion on the process of learning from failure and using it as a catalyst for future success:

1. **Embracing a Growth Mindset:**

   - **Understanding Failure as a Learning Opportunity:** Adopting a growth mindset involves viewing failure not as a permanent setback but as an opportunity for growth and learning. Individuals with a growth mindset believe that their abilities can be developed through dedication and hard work.

- **Fostering Resilience:** Embracing failure with resilience allows individuals to bounce back from setbacks. Resilience is the ability to adapt and recover, facing challenges with determination rather than succumbing to discouragement.

2. **Analyzing the Root Causes:**

- **Thorough Reflection:** After experiencing failure, take the time for thorough reflection. Analyze the root causes, identifying factors that contributed to the setback. This process requires honesty and a willingness to confront challenges head-on.

- **Seeking Feedback:** Solicit feedback from mentors, colleagues, or trusted advisors. External perspectives can provide valuable insights and alternative viewpoints that may not be immediately apparent.

### 3. Extracting Lessons and Insights:

- **Identifying Patterns:** Look for patterns or recurring themes in past failures. Identifying commonalities allows individuals to address underlying issues and make informed decisions to avoid similar pitfalls in the future.

- **Extracting Key Lessons:** Every failure holds valuable lessons. Determine what went wrong, what worked, and how to apply these lessons moving forward. Understanding the nuances of the failure contributes to a more informed and resilient approach.

### 4. Cultivating a Positive Mindset:

- **Reframing Failure:** Cultivate a positive mindset by reframing failure as a temporary setback rather than a permanent defeat. Recognize that setbacks are inherent to any ambitious journey and are stepping stones toward eventual success.

- **Focusing on Solutions:** Instead of dwelling on the failure itself, shift the focus to solutions and actions that can be taken to overcome challenges. A positive mindset promotes proactive problem-solving.

## 5. Adapting and Iterating:

- **Iterative Approach:** Use failure as an opportunity for iteration. Adopt an iterative approach by refining strategies, processes, or products based on the lessons learned. Each iteration brings the endeavor one step closer to success.

- **Flexibility and Adaptability:** Be flexible and adaptable in the face of failure. The ability to pivot, adjust, and embrace change is crucial for overcoming setbacks and finding alternative pathways to success.

## 6. Setting Realistic Expectations:

- **Reassessing Expectations:** Failure often occurs when expectations are unrealistic or not aligned with the circumstances. Reassess and adjust expectations, ensuring they are grounded in reality and achievable within the given context.

- **Setting Incremental Goals:** Break down larger goals into smaller, more manageable milestones. Achieving incremental success builds confidence and momentum, reducing the risk of overwhelming setbacks.

7. **Building a Support System:**

- **Surrounding Yourself with Supportive Individuals:** Building a support system of friends, mentors, and colleagues provides emotional and practical assistance during challenging times. Share experiences and seek guidance from those who have navigated similar setbacks.

- **Leveraging Mentorship:** A mentor can offer valuable insights and guidance based on their own experiences with failure. Learning from the experiences of others can provide a roadmap for overcoming challenges.

8. **Cultivating Perseverance:**

- **Staying Committed:** Perseverance is the ability to persist in the face of challenges. Stay committed to the larger vision or goal, recognizing that setbacks are temporary obstacles on the journey to success.

- **Developing Grit:** Grit, a combination of passion and perseverance, is a key factor in overcoming failure. Cultivate grit by maintaining a long-term perspective and continuing to work diligently toward objectives.

9.  **Celebrating Small Wins:**

- **Acknowledging Progress:** Celebrate small wins and achievements along the way. Recognizing progress, no matter how incremental reinforces a positive mindset and motivates continued effort.

- **Building Momentum**: Each small success builds momentum, creating a positive feedback loop that counteracts the effects of failure. Momentum is a powerful force in propelling individuals toward larger accomplishments.

10.  **Fearlessly Pursuing Future Opportunities:**

- **Risk-Taking:** Learning from failure involves a willingness to take calculated risks. Fearlessly pursue future opportunities, armed with the insights gained from past setbacks and a commitment to continuous improvement.

- **Innovation and Creativity:** Failure often sparks innovation and creativity. Use the lessons learned to explore new approaches, challenge the status quo, and discover novel solutions to problems.

## 11. Maintaining a Long-Term Perspective:

- **Long-Term Vision:** Maintain a long-term perspective when navigating failure. Understand that setbacks are temporary, and success is often a result of perseverance and the ability to learn and adapt over time.

- **Resilience Over Time:** Resilience is not a one-time event but a characteristic developed over time. Embrace failure as an integral part of the journey, knowing that each setback contributes to the resilience needed for long-term success.

In conclusion, the process of learning from failure involves a combination of mindset shifts, reflective analysis, adaptation, and perseverance. By approaching failure as a teacher rather than an adversary, individuals can transform setbacks into valuable lessons and use them as stepping stones toward greater success. The journey from failure to success is not linear, but with a resilient and adaptable mindset, individuals can navigate challenges with newfound strength and wisdom.

## - Adapting to Market Changes and Economic Shifts

Adapting to market changes and economic shifts is a critical process for individuals, businesses, and organizations aiming to thrive in dynamic and ever-evolving environments. Economic landscapes are subject to fluctuations influenced by various factors, including technological advancements, geopolitical events, and shifts in consumer behavior. Here is a comprehensive discussion on the process of adapting to market changes and economic shifts:

1. **Continuous Environmental Monitoring:**

   - **Market Research and Analysis:** Regularly conduct market research to stay informed about industry trends, consumer preferences, and competitive landscapes. Continuous analysis provides insights into emerging opportunities and potential threats.

   - **Economic Indicators:** Monitor economic indicators such as inflation rates, interest rates, and employment figures. These indicators offer valuable signals about broader economic shifts that can impact markets.

2. **Agility and Flexibility:**

   - **Organizational Agility:** Cultivate organizational agility to respond promptly to market changes. This involves creating a flexible and responsive structure that can adapt quickly to shifting circumstances.

- **Iterative Decision-Making:** Adopt an iterative approach to decision-making. Regularly reassess strategies, products, and services based on market feedback, and be willing to pivot when necessary.

3. **Scenario Planning:**

- **Risk Assessment:** Engage in scenario planning to identify potential risks and challenges associated with market changes. Assess the impact of various economic scenarios on the business and develop contingency plans accordingly.

- **Strategic Responses**: Plan strategic responses for different scenarios, considering both short-term adjustments and long-term strategic shifts. Anticipating potential changes allows for proactive adaptation.

4. **Customer-Centric Approach**:

- **Understanding Customer Needs:** Stay attuned to changing customer needs and expectations. Regularly gather feedback, conduct surveys, and monitor customer behavior to identify shifts in preferences and priorities.

- **Personalization and Innovation:** Personalize products or services based on evolving customer preferences. Embrace innovation to create offerings that align with market trends and address emerging demands.

5. **Investment in Technology:**

- **Digital Transformation:** Invest in technology to facilitate digital transformation. Embrace automation, data analytics, and other technological advancements to enhance operational efficiency and adapt to changing market dynamics.

- **E-commerce and Online Presence:** Strengthen the online presence and e-commerce capabilities. The digital landscape is integral to modern business, and an effective online strategy is crucial for reaching and engaging with customers.

6. **Supply Chain Optimization:**

- **Diversification and Resilience:** Optimize supply chains by diversifying sources and creating resilient networks. Economic shifts can impact supply chain dynamics, and a robust, adaptable supply chain is essential for mitigating disruptions.

- **Inventory Management:** Implement effective inventory management practices. Balancing inventory levels with demand fluctuations helps prevent overstocking or shortages, optimizing operational efficiency.

7. **Strategic Partnerships and Collaborations:**

- **Partnership Development:** Form strategic partnerships with other businesses, suppliers, or industry stakeholders. Collaborative efforts can create synergies and provide mutual support during economic shifts.

- **Industry Alliances:** Join industry alliances or associations to stay informed about industry trends and collaborate on addressing common challenges. Shared insights and resources enhance adaptability.

8. **Financial Resilience and Risk Management:**

- **Diverse Revenue Streams:** Develop diverse revenue streams to reduce reliance on a single source. A diversified income portfolio provides financial resilience during economic uncertainties.

   - **Effective Risk Management:** Implement effective risk management practices, including hedging strategies, insurance coverage, and financial contingency planning. Managing financial risks helps buffer against economic volatility.

9.  **Talent Development and Retention:**

   - **Continuous Skill Development:** Invest in continuous skill development for employees to keep pace with evolving market demands. A skilled and adaptable workforce is a valuable asset during economic shifts.

   - **Talent Retention Strategies:** Implement strategies to retain top talent. Experienced and adaptable employees play a crucial role in navigating market changes and contributing to organizational resilience.

## 10. Regulatory Compliance and Adaptation:

- **Regulatory Monitoring:** Stay updated on regulatory changes that may impact the industry. Compliance with evolving regulations is essential for avoiding legal challenges and adapting to market conditions.

- **Advocacy and Engagement:** Engage with regulatory bodies and industry associations to advocate for policies that support business adaptability. Proactive involvement can influence favorable regulatory environments.

## 11. Communication and Stakeholder Engagement:

- **Transparent Communication:** Maintain transparent communication with stakeholders, including customers, employees, investors, and suppliers. Open dialogue fosters trust and keeps stakeholders informed during periods of change.

- **Engagement Strategies:** Develop engagement strategies to keep stakeholders involved in the adaptation process. Inclusion and collaboration enhance support and alignment with organizational goals.

## 12. Learning Culture and Adaptation Feedback Loops:

- **Encouraging a Learning Culture:** Foster a culture of continuous learning within the organization. Encourage employees to adapt, acquire new skills, and contribute to the organization's overall adaptability.

- **Feedback Mechanisms:** Establish feedback mechanisms for employees and customers. Regularly collect feedback on products, services, and processes to identify areas for improvement and adaptation.

## 13. Crisis Management and Contingency Planning:

- **Comprehensive Crisis Management:** Develop comprehensive crisis management plans that include specific responses to economic downturns or market disruptions. Preparedness minimizes the impact of unforeseen challenges.

- **Regular Plan Reviews:** Regularly review and update crisis management and contingency plans. Adapting plans based on evolving circumstances ensures relevance and effectiveness during times of crisis.

14. **Global Market Considerations:**

- **Globalization Strategies:** If applicable, consider globalization strategies. Expanding into international markets can provide diversification and access to new opportunities, but it also requires understanding and adapting to diverse economic landscapes.

- **Geo-Political Considerations:** Stay informed about geopolitical events that may impact global markets. Adaptation strategies should account for the potential effects of political shifts and international relations.

15. **Sustainability and Social Responsibility:**

- **Sustainable Practices:** Embrace sustainable business practices. Market changes are increasingly influenced by environmental, social, and governance (ESG) factors. Sustainability initiatives contribute to long-term resilience and positive brand perception.

- **Corporate Social Responsibility (CSR):** Engage in CSR activities that align with market expectations. Being socially responsible enhances brand reputation and contributes to positive stakeholder relationships.

In conclusion, adapting to market changes and economic shifts is a multifaceted process that requires continuous monitoring, strategic planning, and a proactive mindset. Successful adaptation involves a combination of agility, innovation, risk management, and a commitment to ongoing learning. By implementing these strategies and embracing change as an inherent part of the business landscape, individuals and organizations can navigate economic shifts with resilience and position themselves for sustained success.

## - Building Emotional Resilience for Long-Term Success

Building emotional resilience is a transformative process that equips individuals with the mental and emotional fortitude to navigate challenges, setbacks, and uncertainties. Emotional resilience is crucial for long-term success as it enables individuals to bounce back from adversity, adapt to change, and maintain well-being amidst life's inevitable ups and downs. Here's a comprehensive discussion on the process of building emotional resilience for long-term success:

1. **Self-Awareness and Emotional Intelligence:**

   - **Understanding Emotions:** The foundation of emotional resilience begins with self-awareness.

Understand and acknowledge your emotions, recognizing their impact on thoughts and behaviors.

- **Developing Emotional Intelligence:** Cultivate emotional intelligence by enhancing your ability to perceive, understand, and manage emotions, both in yourself and others. Emotional intelligence is key to responding effectively to challenging situations.

2.  **Positive Mindset and Optimism:**

- **Cultivating a Positive Outlook:** Adopt a positive mindset by focusing on solutions rather than dwelling on problems. Cultivate optimism by viewing challenges as opportunities for growth and learning.

- **Gratitude Practices:** Incorporate gratitude practices into your routine. Expressing gratitude fosters a positive mindset and helps shift the focus from what's lacking to what's present.

3.  **Adaptability and Flexibility:**

- **Embracing Change:** Build resilience by embracing change as a natural part of life. Develop an adaptable and flexible mindset, understanding that the ability to pivot in the face of adversity is a strength.

   - **Iterative Problem-Solving:** Approach challenges with an iterative problem-solving mindset. Break down problems into manageable steps, reassess solutions as needed, and adjust strategies based on feedback.

## 4. Building a Strong Support System:

   - **Connection with Others:** Foster connections with friends, family, mentors, and colleagues. A strong support system provides emotional support, perspective, and a sense of belonging during challenging times.

   - **Effective Communication:** Develop effective communication skills to express emotions and seek support. Open communication builds trust and strengthens relationships, contributing to emotional resilience.

5.  **Mindfulness and Stress Management:**

- **Practicing Mindfulness:** Engage in mindfulness practices, such as meditation or deep breathing exercises. Mindfulness enhances self-awareness, reduces stress, and promotes emotional balance.

- **Stress Reduction Techniques:** Learn and apply stress reduction techniques, including time management, prioritization, and setting boundaries. Managing stress proactively prevents its detrimental impact on emotional resilience.

6.  **Coping Strategies and Emotional Regulation:**

- **Healthy Coping Mechanisms:** Develop healthy coping mechanisms for dealing with stress and challenges. This may include engaging in hobbies, physical exercise, or creative outlets to channel and release emotional energy.

- **Emotional Regulation:** Practice emotional regulation by learning to manage intense emotions effectively. Techniques such as deep breathing, journaling, or seeking professional guidance contribute to emotional stability.

7.  **Building Confidence and Self-Efficacy:**

 - **Setting Realistic Goals:** Build confidence by setting realistic and achievable goals. Celebrate small victories, and gradually tackle more significant challenges to enhance a sense of self-efficacy.

 - **Learning from Setbacks:** View setbacks as opportunities for learning and growth. Each failure or challenge can contribute to personal development and the strengthening of emotional resilience.

8.  **Continuous Learning and Adaptation:**

 - **Learning Orientation:** Adopt a learning orientation by seeing challenges as opportunities to acquire new skills and knowledge. The willingness to learn and adapt contributes to resilience in the face of evolving circumstances.

 - **Adapting to Feedback:** Be open to feedback and constructive criticism. Use feedback as a tool for improvement, refining your approach based on lessons learned from both successes and failures.

9.  **Developing a Sense of Purpose:**

- **Clarifying Values and Purpose:** Cultivate a sense of purpose by clarifying your values and long-term goals. Aligning actions with a meaningful purpose provides a sense of direction and resilience during challenging times.

- **Contributing to Others:** Engage in activities that contribute to the well-being of others. Acts of kindness and service create a sense of purpose and foster a positive, resilient mindset.

10.  **Time Management and Boundaries:**

- **Effective Time Management:** Manage time effectively by prioritizing tasks and setting realistic deadlines. Proactively addressing time-related stressors contributes to emotional resilience.

- **Setting Boundaries:** Establish and communicate personal and professional boundaries. Knowing when to say no and setting limits on commitments prevents overwhelm and burnout, promoting emotional well-being.

11. **Reflection and Mindset Growth:**

- **Reflective Practices:** Engage in reflective practices to assess experiences and emotions. Regular self-reflection enhances self-awareness and facilitates mindset growth.

- **Learning from Challenges:** Develop a growth mindset by seeing challenges as opportunities to learn and improve. Embrace a belief that abilities can be developed through dedication and effort.

12. **Professional Guidance and Support:**

- **Therapeutic Support:** Seek professional guidance when needed. Therapists, counsellors, or mental health professionals can provide valuable insights, coping strategies, and emotional support.

- **Coaching and Mentorship:** Engage in coaching or mentorship relationships. Experienced mentors can share insights, offer guidance, and serve as role models for building emotional resilience.

13. **Celebrating Resilience Milestones:**

- **Acknowledging Progress:** Celebrate milestones in your journey of building emotional resilience. Recognizing and acknowledging progress reinforces positive behaviors and contributes to a sense of accomplishment.

- **Self-Compassion:** Practice self-compassion during challenging times. Treat yourself with the same kindness and understanding that you would offer to a friend facing difficulties.

14. **Balancing Work and Life:**

- **Work-Life Balance**: Strive for a healthy work-life balance. Allocating time for personal life, relaxation, and rejuvenation is crucial for sustaining emotional resilience over the long term.

- **Setting Realistic Expectations:** Manage expectations realistically, both in personal and professional domains. Setting achievable goals reduces the risk of stress and burnout.

15. **Community Engagement and Social Connection:**

- **Community Involvement:** Engage with communities and social groups. Building connections outside of work or immediate family provides a broader support network and contributes to emotional resilience.

- **Social Connection Practices:** Foster social connections through regular interactions, whether in person or virtually. Shared experiences and connections contribute to a sense of belonging and emotional well-being.

In conclusion, building emotional resilience is a multifaceted and ongoing process that involves self-awareness, positive mindset cultivation, adaptive strategies, and a commitment to continuous learning. By incorporating these practices into daily life, individuals can strengthen their emotional resilience, fostering the mental and emotional fortitude needed for long-term success in both personal and professional spheres.

# CHAPTER 5: BEYOND MONEY: CREATING A HOLISTIC ABUNDANT LIFE

Welcome to the transformative journey of "Beyond Money: Creating a Holistic Abundant Life," a chapter that invites you to explore the dimensions of wealth that extend far beyond monetary measures. In the pursuit of a fulfilling and prosperous life, it's essential to recognize that abundance encompasses more than financial success. This chapter delves into the multifaceted aspects of holistic well-being, fostering a mindset that values not only monetary wealth but also personal growth, relationships, health, and a sense of purpose.

In a world often fixated on financial metrics, this chapter challenges the conventional notion of prosperity, urging you to consider the richness found in various facets of life. True abundance involves a harmonious blend of material wealth, emotional well-being, and a profound connection to one's passions and purpose.

Through these pages, you will embark on a journey of self-discovery and exploration, learning how to cultivate abundance in diverse areas of your life. Whether it's nurturing meaningful relationships, prioritizing mental and physical health, or aligning with your core values, the chapters ahead provide insights, practical strategies, and inspiration to help you create a life rich in fulfilment

Prepare to transcend the narrow confines of monetary wealth and embrace a holistic perspective on abundance. As we navigate the terrain of "Beyond Money," you'll uncover the keys to unlocking a life that is not just financially prosperous but also deeply meaningful, satisfying, and abundant in every sense. Welcome to a chapter that encourages you to redefine success and design a life that reflects your unique vision of holistic abundance.

# - Balancing Work and Personal Life for Fulfillment

Balancing work and personal life is a dynamic and ongoing process that requires intentional effort and mindful choices to achieve fulfilment in both areas. Achieving a harmonious balance ensures that individuals can meet professional responsibilities while also nurturing their personal well-being, relationships, and passions. Here's a comprehensive discussion on the process of balancing work and personal life for fulfilment:

1. **Clarifying Values and Priorities:**

   - **Identifying Core Values:** Begin by identifying your core values. What matters most to you in both your personal and professional life? Understanding your values serves as a foundation for making decisions that align with your priorities.

- **Establishing Priorities:** Prioritize your values and commitments. Recognize that not every task or opportunity is of equal importance. Clearly defining priorities helps in making informed choices about how to allocate time and energy.

2. **Setting Realistic Expectations:**

- **Managing Expectations:** Set realistic expectations for both work and personal life. Understand the demands and expectations in your professional role and communicate openly with colleagues, superiors, and family members about realistic timeframes and commitments.

- **Avoiding Perfectionism:** Embrace the idea that perfection is unattainable. Strive for excellence, but understand that it's okay not to excel in every aspect of work and personal life simultaneously.

3. **Effective Time Management:**

- **Prioritization and Planning:** Practice effective time management by prioritizing tasks and creating a realistic schedule. Plan your work and personal activities, allocating dedicated time for both to avoid overlap and reduce stress.

- **Time Blocking:** Consider implementing time-blocking techniques, where specific blocks of time are dedicated to work, family, personal development, and leisure. This helps maintain focus on one aspect without distractions from another.

4. **Establishing Boundaries:**

- **Work-Life Boundaries:** Clearly define boundaries between work and personal life. Establish set working hours, and when the workday ends, commit to disengaging from professional responsibilities to focus on personal pursuits and relationships.

- **Communication Boundaries:** Communicate your boundaries effectively. Inform colleagues and family members about your availability and establish expectations for when you can be reached and when you need dedicated personal time.

## 5. Self-Care Practices:

- **Prioritizing Self-Care:** Make self-care a non-negotiable part of your routine. This includes activities that rejuvenate your physical and mental well-being, such as exercise, meditation, adequate sleep, and hobbies.

- **Regular Breaks:** Incorporate short breaks during the workday to refresh your mind. These breaks can contribute to increased productivity and focus, ultimately benefiting both your work and personal life.

## 6. Flexible Work Arrangements:

- **Exploring Flexibility:** Explore flexible work arrangements, such as remote work or flexible hours. Many workplaces offer options that allow employees to better balance work and personal commitments.

- **Negotiating Terms:** If possible, negotiate terms that support work-life balance. This may include discussing reduced hours, compressed workweeks, or job-sharing arrangements that align with both personal and professional goals.

7.  **Quality over Quantity Time:**

- **Prioritizing Quality Time:** Recognize the importance of quality time over quantity. Whether at work or with family, focus on being present and fully engaged during the time you allocate to each aspect of your life.

- **Limiting Distractions:** Minimize distractions during quality time by turning off electronic devices, creating designated spaces for work and personal activities, and setting clear expectations for uninterrupted moments.

8.  **Regular Check-Ins and Adjustments:**

- **Reflective Practices:** Regularly reflect on your work-life balance. Assess whether your current approach aligns with your values and priorities.

Adjust your strategies if needed to ensure an ongoing balance that fosters fulfilment.

 - **Feedback and Communication:** Solicit feedback from family members, friends, and colleagues regarding your availability and effectiveness in both spheres. Open communication allows for adjustments based on evolving needs and expectations.

9.  **Outsourcing and Delegating Responsibilities:**

 - **Delegating Tasks:** Delegate tasks at work and home when possible. Empower colleagues and family members to share responsibilities, reducing the burden on any single individual and creating a more balanced distribution of tasks.

 - **Outsourcing Services**: Consider outsourcing tasks that do not align with your core responsibilities or bring you joy. Services like house cleaning, grocery delivery, or virtual assistance can free up time for more meaningful activities.

## 10. Aligning Career Goals with Personal Values:

**- Reflecting on Career Alignment:** Assess whether your current career aligns with your values and goals. If there's a misalignment, explore opportunities or career paths that better resonate with your overall life aspirations.

**- Negotiating Work Expectations:** If necessary, negotiate with employers about adjustments to your workload or responsibilities. Many organizations value employee well-being and are open to finding solutions that benefit both parties.

## 11. Building Support Networks:

**- Seeking Support:** Build a support network both at work and in your personal life. Seek guidance from mentors, colleagues, friends, and family members who can offer insights, share experiences, and provide emotional support.

**- Networking for Work-Life Balance:** Engage with professional networks or organizations that prioritize work-life balance. Sharing experiences and best practices with like-minded individuals can offer valuable perspectives and strategies.

## 12. Continuous Learning and Adaptation:

- **Embracing Lifelong Learning:** Embrace a mindset of continuous learning and adaptation. The dynamics of work and personal life are constantly evolving, and being open to learning new strategies ensures ongoing success in balancing both spheres.

- **Adjusting Strategies:** Be willing to adjust your strategies as circumstances change. Life stages, career developments, and personal priorities may shift, requiring periodic reassessment and adaptation of your work-life balance approach.

## 13. Celebrating Achievements:

- **Acknowledging Milestones:** Celebrate achievements in both your professional and personal life. Acknowledging milestones, whether

big or small, contributes to a sense of
accomplishment and reinforces the positive aspects
of work and personal endeavors.

  - **Balancing Recognition:** Strive for a balance in
recognizing achievements in both spheres. Avoiding
the dominance of one aspect over the other
contributes to a holistic sense of fulfilment.

14.  **Modeling Healthy Balance for Others:**

If applicable, model a healthy work-life balance
for colleagues, subordinates, and family members.
Demonstrating the importance of fulfilment in both
areas contributes to a positive workplace culture
and family dynamic.

  - **Educating and Advocating:** Share your
experiences and insights about work-life balance
with others. Educate colleagues, friends, and family
about the benefits of balance and advocate for
supportive environments that enable individuals to
thrive in both realms.

15. **Seeking Professional Guidance:**

- **Career and Life Coaches:** Consider seeking guidance from career and life coaches. Professionals in these fields can offer personalized strategies, insights, and support in navigating the complexities of balancing work and personal life.

- **Mental Health Support:** If feelings of imbalance persist, seek the guidance of mental health professionals. They can provide tools for managing stress, anxiety, and other challenges that may hinder the achievement of a fulfilling work-life balance.

In conclusion, the process of balancing work and personal life for fulfilment is a holistic and adaptive journey. By integrating these strategies into your daily life, you can cultivate a harmonious balance that promotes well-being, satisfaction, and success in both professional and personal spheres. Remember that achieving balance is an ongoing process, and flexibility and self-awareness are key components in navigating the dynamic interplay between work and personal life.

# - The Importance of Giving Back: Philanthropy and Social Impact

The importance of giving back through philanthropy and social impact is profound, as it plays a pivotal role in creating positive change and fostering a more equitable and compassionate society. Philanthropy goes beyond financial donations; it encompasses the intentional efforts to contribute time, resources, and expertise to address pressing social issues. Here's a comprehensive discussion on the significance of giving back and its impact on individuals, communities, and society at large:

1. **Addressing Social Issues:**

- **Tackling Inequities:** Philanthropy catalyzes addressing systemic inequities and social injustices. By supporting initiatives that target poverty, education gaps, healthcare disparities, and other challenges, philanthropy becomes a driving force for positive change.

- **Supporting Vulnerable Populations:** Philanthropic efforts often focus on assisting vulnerable populations, including those affected by poverty, homelessness, discrimination, or natural disasters. These initiatives contribute to building a more inclusive and compassionate society.

2. **Empowering Communities:**

- **Community Development:** Philanthropy empowers communities by supporting local development projects, infrastructure improvements, and initiatives that enhance the overall well-being of residents. This empowerment fosters self-sufficiency and community resilience.

- **Capacity Building:** Investing in community organizations and grassroots movements builds their capacity to create lasting impact. Philanthropic support enables these entities to develop sustainable solutions tailored to the unique needs of their communities.

## 3. Advancing Education:

- **Educational Opportunities:** Philanthropy plays a key role in advancing education by supporting scholarships, building schools, and providing resources for quality learning environments. Access to education is a powerful tool for breaking the cycle of poverty and fostering individual empowerment.

- **STEM and Skill Development:** Philanthropic efforts often target science, technology, engineering, and mathematics (STEM) education, as well as vocational training. These initiatives prepare individuals for the evolving demands of the workforce and contribute to economic development.

## 4. Health and Well-Being:

- **Medical Research and Access:** Philanthropy supports medical research, healthcare infrastructure, and initiatives that enhance access to healthcare services. These efforts contribute to advancements in medical treatments, disease prevention, and improved overall health outcomes.

- **Mental Health Initiatives:** The importance of mental health is increasingly recognized in philanthropy. Initiatives supporting mental health awareness, counselling services, and DE stigmatization contribute to a more holistic approach to well-being.

5. **Environmental Stewardship:**

- **Conservation and Sustainability:** Philanthropy plays a critical role in supporting environmental conservation and sustainability efforts. Funding projects that protect natural habitats, promote renewable energy, and address climate change contributes to the well-being of the planet and future generations.

- **Biodiversity Preservation:** Initiatives that focus on preserving biodiversity and ecosystems are often backed by philanthropic support. These efforts contribute to maintaining a balanced and resilient natural environment.

6. **Humanitarian Aid and Crisis Response:**

- **Disaster Relief:** Philanthropy swiftly responds to humanitarian crises by providing disaster relief, including food, shelter, and medical aid. This immediate assistance is crucial in mitigating the impact of natural disasters, conflicts, and emergencies.

- **Refugee Support:** Philanthropy supports programs that aid refugees and displaced populations, offering assistance with resettlement, education, and access to necessities. These initiatives contribute to rebuilding lives in the aftermath of displacement.

7. **Social Innovation and Entrepreneurship:**

- **Fostering Innovation:** Philanthropy often supports social entrepreneurship and innovation. Funding for ventures that address social challenges through creative and sustainable solutions contributes to positive societal transformation.

- **Impact Investing:** The rise of impact investing, where philanthropic capital is used to generate both social and financial returns, highlights the potential for aligning business practices with social impact goals.

8. **Promoting Cultural and Artistic Expression:**

- **Cultural Preservation:** Philanthropy contributes to the preservation of cultural heritage, supporting initiatives that safeguard historical sites, artefacts, and traditions. Cultural preservation fosters a sense of identity and connection within communities.

- **Arts and Creativity:** Supporting the arts through philanthropy enhances cultural enrichment and creative expression. Funding for museums, theatres, and artistic programs contributes to a vibrant and diverse cultural landscape.

## 9. Building Social Cohesion:

- **Fostering Inclusivity:** Philanthropy promotes inclusivity by supporting initiatives that celebrate diversity and advocate for equal rights. These efforts contribute to building social cohesion and fostering a sense of belonging for all members of society.

- **Community Engagement:** Philanthropy encourages community engagement and participation in social issues. Through volunteerism and grassroots involvement, individuals become active contributors to positive change within their communities.

## 10. Inspiring Social Responsibility:

- **Corporate Social Responsibility (CSR):** Philanthropy is integral to corporate social responsibility, where businesses actively contribute to societal well-being. CSR initiatives demonstrate a commitment to ethical practices, sustainability, and positive social impact.

- **Individual Responsibility:** Philanthropy inspires individuals to recognize their role in creating positive change. It encourages a sense of social responsibility, motivating people to contribute to the well-being of their communities through various means.

## 11.  Creating Lasting Legacies:

- **Endowments and Foundations:** Philanthropy often involves the establishment of endowments and foundations. These entities can create lasting legacies by providing ongoing support for causes that align with the donor's values and vision.

- **Impact beyond a Lifetime:** Philanthropic contributions have the potential to transcend an individual's lifetime, leaving a positive and enduring impact on society. This legacy reflects a commitment to creating a better future for generations to come.

## 12. Global Collaboration:

- International Aid: Philanthropy extends beyond national borders to address global challenges. International aid and collaboration foster a sense of interconnectedness, as philanthropists contribute to solving issues that impact people worldwide.

- **Partnerships and Networks:** Philanthropy encourages collaboration between governments, non-profit organizations, businesses, and individuals. These partnerships amplify the impact of efforts to address complex global issues.

## 13. Measuring Impact and Accountability:

- **Impact Assessment:** Philanthropy increasingly emphasizes the importance of measuring impact. Rigorous evaluation and assessment help philanthropists understand the effectiveness of their contributions and make informed decisions for future initiatives.

- **Transparency and Accountability:** Philanthropic organizations strive for transparency and accountability in their operations. Communicating goals, outcomes, and financial allocations builds trust with donors and beneficiaries alike.

## 14. Educating and Raising Awareness:

- **Philanthropy Education:** Philanthropy contributes to educational initiatives that promote awareness about social issues and the role individuals can play in creating positive change. Philanthropy education fosters a culture of giving and empathy.

- **Advocacy and Social Movements:** Philanthropy supports advocacy efforts and social movements. By funding campaigns and initiatives that raise awareness, philanthropy contributes to societal shifts in attitudes and policies.

## 15. Personal Fulfillment and Well-Being:

- **Sense of Purpose:** Engaging in philanthropy provides individuals with a sense of purpose and fulfilment. Knowing that one's contributions make a positive impact on the lives of others contributes to overall well-being.

  **- Connection and Empathy:** Philanthropy nurtures a sense of connection and empathy. Understanding the needs of others and actively working to address those needs fosters a deeper appreciation for the interconnectedness of humanity.

In conclusion, the importance of giving back through philanthropy and social impact is multifaceted, touching on various aspects of societal well-being and positive transformation. Whether addressing pressing social issues, empowering communities, or fostering cultural enrichment, philanthropy plays a crucial role in creating a more equitable, compassionate, and sustainable world. By recognizing the significance of giving back, individuals and organizations can actively contribute to building a better future for all.

# - Legacy Building: Ensuring Your Wealth Endures Through Generations

Legacy building is a strategic and intentional process that goes beyond financial wealth, aiming to ensure that an individual's values, accomplishments, and resources endure and positively impact future generations. Crafting a lasting legacy involves thoughtful planning, values-based decision-making, and a commitment to leaving a meaningful imprint on the world. Here's a comprehensive discussion on legacy building, encompassing financial and non-financial aspects to ensure that wealth endures through generations:

1. **Defining Personal Values and Vision:**

   - **Identifying Core Values:** Legacy building starts with a clear understanding of personal values.

Identify the principles and beliefs that define your life and the legacy you wish to leave behind.

- **Vision for the Future**: Envision the impact you want to have on future generations. Consider the values, skills, and experiences you hope to pass on and the positive changes you wish to inspire.

2. **Holistic Wealth Planning:**

- **Financial Planning:** While financial wealth is a crucial component, legacy planning extends beyond traditional financial strategies. Develop a comprehensive financial plan that aligns with your long-term vision, including investments, estate planning, and wealth preservation.

- **Non-Financial Assets:** Identify non-financial assets that contribute to your legacy, such as intellectual property, family traditions, stories, and personal accomplishments. These assets are integral to conveying your values and life lessons.

3. **Educating and Empowering Heirs:**

- **Financial Literacy:** Prioritize the education of heirs about financial matters. Equip them with the knowledge and skills needed to manage wealth responsibly, make informed decisions, and sustain the family's financial well-being.

- **Values Transmission:** Beyond financial education, instill your values in heirs. Share stories, experiences, and the principles that shaped your life. This values transmission is essential for maintaining a strong family identity and cohesion.

4. **Estate Planning and Asset Protection:**

- **Structured Estate Plans:** Develop a well-structured estate plan that aligns with your legacy goals. This includes wills, trusts, and other legal instruments to ensure a smooth transfer of assets and minimize potential disputes.

- **Asset Protection Strategies:** Implement strategies to protect assets from potential risks, such as legal liabilities, taxes, or economic downturns. Proper asset protection enhances the sustainability of wealth through generations.

5. **Philanthropy and Social Impact:**

- **Establishing Family Foundations:** Consider establishing a family foundation or charitable trust as part of your legacy plan. These entities can perpetuate your commitment to philanthropy, allowing your wealth to contribute to a positive social impact.

- **Teaching Generosity:** Instill a sense of social responsibility and philanthropy in your family. Engage heirs in charitable activities, involve them in decision-making for charitable contributions, and teach the importance of giving back to the community.

6. **Business Succession Planning:**

- **Succession Strategies:** If you have a family business, develop a clear succession plan. Ensure a smooth transition of leadership and ownership, taking into account the skills, values, and aspirations of the next generation.

- **Family Governance:** Establish family governance structures, such as family councils or boards, to facilitate effective communication, decision-making, and conflict resolution within the family business context.

## 7. Preserving Family Traditions and Stories:

- **Oral Histories:** Preserve family traditions and stories through oral histories. Share personal experiences, challenges overcome, and the values that have shaped the family. This storytelling tradition fosters a sense of identity and connection.

- **Documenting Family History:** Consider creating a family archive or history book. Documenting the family's journey, achievements, and the lessons learned provides a tangible legacy that can be passed down through generations.

## 8. Mentoring and Leadership Development:

- **Mentorship Programs:** Establish mentorship programs within the family to pass on knowledge, skills, and values. Encourage experienced family members to mentor younger generations in areas such as business, leadership, and life skills.

- **Leadership Training:** Provide opportunities for family members to develop leadership skills. This may include formal education, training programs, or exposure to real-world experiences that prepare them to take on leadership roles in the family and beyond.

9. **Environmental and Social Responsibility:**

- **Sustainable Practices:** Integrate environmentally sustainable practices into your legacy. Consider investments and initiatives that promote environmental stewardship, addressing issues such as climate change and resource conservation.

- **Social Responsibility:** Embrace a commitment to social responsibility by aligning your legacy with ethical business practices and social impact initiatives. Encourage family members to prioritize values-driven decision-making in their personal and professional lives.

10.  Creating a Family Constitution:

  - **Defining Family Values:** Draft a family constitution or mission statement that articulates the core values, vision, and purpose of the family. This document serves as a guiding framework for future generations, ensuring continuity in family values.

  - **Conflict Resolution Protocols:** Include conflict resolution protocols in the family constitution to address potential disputes. Clearly defined processes for resolving conflicts contribute to family unity and the sustainability of your legacy.

11.  **Regular Family Meetings and Communication:**

  - **Open Communication:** Foster open and transparent communication within the family. Regular family meetings provide opportunities to discuss goals, address concerns, and reinforce shared values, ensuring everyone feels heard and connected.

   - **Inclusive Decision-Making:** Involve family members in decision-making processes related to the family's wealth and legacy. Inclusivity promotes a sense of ownership and commitment to sustaining the family's values and vision.

12.  **Adapting to Changing Circumstances:**

   - **Flexibility in Planning:** Recognize the need for flexibility in legacy planning. Economic, social, and cultural landscapes evolve, and being adaptable allows your legacy plan to adjust to changing circumstances while staying true to its core values.

   - **Periodic Reviews:** Periodically review and update your legacy plan to reflect changes in family dynamics, financial circumstances, and societal trends. Regular evaluations ensure the continued relevance and effectiveness of your legacy-building strategies.

## 13. Professional Guidance and Collaboration:

- **Engaging Professionals:** Seek the guidance of professionals, including estate planners, financial advisors, and legal experts, to develop and implement your legacy plan. Their expertise ensures that your strategies align with legal requirements and best practices.

- **Collaboration with Advisors:** Encourage collaboration between family members and external advisors. Working together with professionals fosters a holistic approach to legacy building, leveraging diverse perspectives and expertise.

## 14. Cultivating a Values-Driven Culture:

- **Leading by Example:** Cultivate a values-driven culture by leading by example. Demonstrate the importance of integrity, resilience, and ethical behavior in both personal and professional spheres.

- **Encouraging Accountability:** Foster a culture of accountability within the family. Encourage family members to hold themselves and each other accountable for upholding the values that form the foundation of the family legacy.

15. **Documenting and Sharing Wisdom**:

- **Wisdom Documents:** Create documents or recordings that capture your wisdom, life lessons, and insights. Share your reflections on success, challenges, and the principles that guided your journey. These documents become valuable resources for future generations.

- **Encouraging Dialogue:** Facilitate open discussions about family values and personal experiences. Encourage family members to share their perspectives, contributing to a collective pool of wisdom that enriches the family's legacy.

In conclusion, legacy building is a dynamic and multifaceted process that requires careful consideration of financial, cultural, and interpersonal factors. By integrating these strategies into your legacy plan, you can create a lasting impact that transcends generations, ensuring that your wealth endures in a meaningful and positive way. The key lies in fostering a values-driven culture, promoting education and empowerment, and adapting to the evolving needs and aspirations of your family over time.

# CONCLUSION

In concluding "The Millionaire Mindset: How to Think and Act like the Rich," I invite you to reflect on the transformative journey we've undertaken together. Throughout these pages, we've explored the principles, strategies, and mindset shifts that distinguish the wealthy and successful. The essence of this book lies not only in accumulating financial wealth but also in cultivating a holistic and empowered approach to life.

As we close this chapter, remember that the path to financial success is intertwined with personal growth, resilience, and a commitment to continuous learning. The millionaire mindset goes beyond monetary gains; it's about adopting a mentality that embraces challenges as opportunities, seeks knowledge voraciously, and values the importance of giving back to the community.

In your hands, you hold more than a guide to financial prosperity; you possess a roadmap to a life rich in purpose, impact, and fulfilment. The journey to wealth is not solely about accumulating assets but also about leaving a positive legacy, nurturing meaningful relationships, and making a difference in the lives of others.

Embrace the mindset of abundance, not just in terms of wealth but in gratitude, generosity, and the willingness to share your success with those around you. Strive for a balance that encompasses financial prosperity, personal well-being, and a deep sense of purpose. As you internalize the principles discussed in these pages, let them serve as the compass guiding you toward a life that reflects the true essence of abundance.

Remember, wealth is not solely measured by the numbers in your bank account but by the impact you make, the relationships you nurture, and the positive change you bring to the world. Cultivate a mindset that sees possibilities where others see obstacles, that embraces challenges as stepping stones to success, and that understands the profound connection between financial prosperity and personal well-being.

May your journey towards the millionaire mindset be a continual exploration, a commitment to lifelong learning, and a testament to the incredible potential that resides within you? As you embark on the path to financial success, may you also find joy, fulfilment, and a sense of purpose that transcends monetary gains?

Thank you for joining me on this journey. May your mindset be forever shaped by the wisdom within these pages, propelling you toward a future of abundance, prosperity, and enduring success? Here's to thinking and acting like the rich – not just in wealth but in every facet of a truly rich and fulfilling life.

www.ingramcontent.com/pod-product-compliance
Lightning Source LLC
Chambersburg PA
CBHW070128260726
48658CB00001B/314